Baby Primates

Bobbie Kalman
Crabtree Publishing Company
www.crabtreebooks.com

It's fun to learn about Baby Animals

Created by Bobbie Kalman

For Freddie,
a most adorable baby primate!

**Author and
Editor-in-Chief**
Bobbie Kalman

Editors
Kathy Middleton
Crystal Sikkens

Photo research
Bobbie Kalman

Design
Bobbie Kalman
Katherine Berti
Samantha Crabtree
  (logo and front cover)

Print and production coordinator
Katherine Berti

Prepress technician
Katherine Berti

Illustrations
Bonna Rouse: pages 8, 24 (skeleton)

Photographs
Creatas: page 9 (top and middle)
Digital Vision: pages 11 (bottom left), 16 (bottom)
Wikimedia Commons: Alex Pyron: pages 7 (bottom
  right), 19 (bottom left)
All other images by Shutterstock

Library and Archives Canada Cataloguing in Publication

Kalman, Bobbie
     Baby primates / Bobbie Kalman.

(It's fun to learn about baby animals)
Includes index.
Issued also in electronic formats.
ISBN 978-0-7787-1007-3 (bound).--ISBN 978-0-7787-1011-0 (pbk.)

     1. Primates--Infancy--Juvenile literature. I. Title. II. Series:
It's fun to learn about baby animals

QL737.P9K24 2013   j599.813'92   C2012-907320-2

Library of Congress Cataloging-in-Publication Data

CIP available at Library of Congress

Crabtree Publishing Company
www.crabtreebooks.com   1-800-387-7650

Printed in Hong Kong/012013/BK20121102

Published in Canada
Crabtree Publishing
616 Welland Ave.
St. Catharines, Ontario
L2M 5V6

Published in the United States
Crabtree Publishing
PMB 59051
350 Fifth Avenue, 59th Floor
New York, New York 10118

Published in the United Kingdom
Crabtree Publishing
Maritime House
Basin Road North, Hove
BN41 1WR

Published in Australia
Crabtree Publishing
3 Charles Street
Coburg North
VIC, 3058

What is in this book?

Primates are the smartest animals on Earth. People are primates, too. Primates are **mammals**. Mammals are animals with hair or fur on their bodies. They grow inside the bodies of their mothers and are **born**. Most mammal mothers, especially primate mothers, take good care of their babies. They keep them safe and teach them how to find food.

This orangutan mother and baby are high up in a tree. Orangutan mothers teach their babies how to climb and leap from tree to tree.

Mother's milk

Mammal mothers feed their babies milk from their bodies. Drinking mother's milk is called **nursing**. Mammal babies nurse soon after they are born. As the babies grow, they nurse less often and start eating the same foods as their parents.

This baby lemur was just born. Its mother is cleaning it with her tongue.

Most primate mothers have one baby at a time, but some, like the lemur mother above, have twins. After a baby lemur is born, it hangs on to its mother's belly and nurses. It is safe there.

5

Kinds of primates

black spider monkey

There are four main groups to which all primates belong. The groups are shown on these pages.

1. Old World monkeys, shown left, are the biggest group of primates. Baboons and macaque monkeys are Old World monkeys (see pages 12–13).

baboons

macaque monkeys

marmoset

2. New World monkeys, shown right, include spider monkeys, marmosets, and tamarins (see pages 14–15).

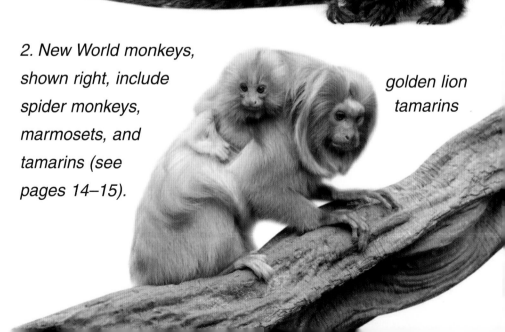

golden lion tamarins

gibbon

bonobo

human baby

orangutan

3. Apes and humans make up another group of primates. Gorillas, gibbons, chimpanzees, bonobos, and orangutans are all apes (see pages 16–17). There is only one **species**, or type, of human.

gorilla

chimpanzee

lemur

4. Lemurs, tarsiers, lorises, and bush babies make up the last group. They are called **prosimians** (see pages 18–19).

tarsier

bush baby

loris

Primate bodies

Primates have arms, legs, hands, and feet, with fingers and toes. Most primates also have thumbs. Primates have big brains, too. They are smart. Like all mammals, primates have a group of bones down the middle of their backs called a **backbone**. All the bones in the body make up the **skeleton**. The skeleton below is a monkey skeleton.

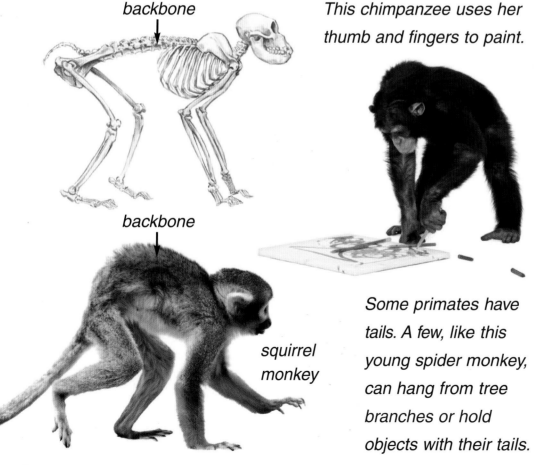

backbone

backbone

squirrel monkey

This chimpanzee uses her thumb and fingers to paint.

Some primates have tails. A few, like this young spider monkey, can hang from tree branches or hold objects with their tails.

8

Warm-blooded

Primates are **warm-blooded**. The body temperature of warm-blooded animals stays about the same in both warm and cold weather.

The body temperature of these macaques stays about the same, whether they are sitting in snow or in a pool of hot water.

Breathing air

Primates have **lungs** for breathing air. Lungs are inside their bodies. They take in air and let out air. This boy **inhales**, or breathes in, air through his nose and into his lungs. He then **exhales**, or breathes out the air.

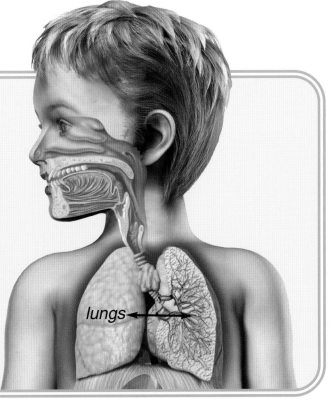

lungs

Primate habitats

Most primates live in forest **habitats**. A habitat is a natural place where an animal lives. Many primates are good climbers and spend most of their time high in trees. They use their strong arms, legs, and feet to climb. Some use their tails, too. Most primates live in warm areas year round, but some live in places that are cold in winter.

Douc langur monkeys live in hot forests in Southeast Asia. This baby is clinging to its mother as she climbs around in the trees, but it will soon learn to climb on its own.

*This mother howler monkey and her baby live in a **rain forest** in South America. It rains every day, and the weather is hot all year.*

Orangutans are apes that live in **jungles**, or hot forests. They live on Borneo and Sumatra, which are islands in Asia. Orangutans spend most of their time in trees and make nests for sleeping.

Mountain gorillas live on the ground in forests that are high on mountains in Africa.

People live all over the world in cities, towns, on mountains, and in forests.

Many kinds of monkeys

Europe
Asia
Southeast Asia
Africa
Madagascar

Old World monkeys make up the largest group of monkeys. There are more than 80 species, or kinds! Old World monkeys live in Africa, Asia, and Europe. Most monkeys live in trees, but a few species live on the ground.

Old World monkeys, like this baby macaque, have nostrils that point forward.

All baboons, like the baby above, have short tails and pads of skin on their bottoms that make sitting comfortable. Baboons live mainly on the ground.

12

Tails, toes, and a big nose

Old World monkeys cannot hold objects with their tails. They hold them with their big toes, fingers, and thumbs. Most Old World monkeys prefer to eat plants, but they also eat insects.

Vervet monkeys live in Africa. The adult monkeys have dark faces and light gray fur, but their babies have pink faces.

Proboscis monkeys are among the largest Old World monkeys. They have big pot bellies, and the males have huge noses! Proboscis monkeys form groups that include one male and several females and their babies.

New World monkeys

North America

Central America

South America

New World monkeys live in Central America and South America. This group includes marmosets and tamarins. New World monkeys live only in trees, and some can hang from branches by their tails. They can use their tails like a hand, but they cannot use their thumbs to hold objects.

The nostrils of these baby capuchins, as well as those of other New World monkeys, point sideways. How are they different from the nostrils of Old World monkeys?

This spider monkey mother and her baby are high up in a rainforest tree. Spider monkeys have long arms and tails. The mother above has wrapped her tail around a tree branch.

Capuchin monkeys are very smart. They are able to use tools and have good memories. They live long lives.

(left) The pygmy marmoset is one of the smallest primates, and the smallest monkey. Its body length is 5.5 to 6.3 inches (14 to 16 cm), not including its long tail.

There are different kinds of tamarins. The one above is a golden lion tamarin. The one on the left is an emperor tamarin.

Great and lesser apes

Gorillas, chimpanzees, bonobos, and orangutans are known as **great apes**. Gibbons are called **lesser apes** because they are smaller and behave more like monkeys. Apes live in Africa and Asia. There are no apes in North America or South America, except in zoos.

Baby gorillas stay close to their mothers until they are between four and five years old. Gorilla mothers and babies live in groups with one male.

Strong animals

Apes are the strongest primates. Most apes are bigger than monkeys. Gorillas are the largest apes. They live on the ground instead of in trees. Gorillas eat fruit, leaves, and flowers. Unlike monkeys, apes have no tails.

Baby orangutans live with their mothers high up in trees. Orangutans do not belong to big groups like other apes do.

Chimpanzees live mainly on the ground, but they sleep in trees. This mother and baby are part of a large **troop**, or group, which can contain from 30 to 80 chimpanzees.

Bonobos are also known as pygmy chimpanzees. Pygmy means small. Bonobos have long legs, pink lips, dark faces, and long hair. This bonobo baby is learning to walk on two legs. Bonobos can walk on two legs for longer periods than other apes can.

Gibbons are lesser apes, which are smaller than great apes and act more like monkeys. They use their long arms to swing from branch to branch and from tree to tree.

On land, gibbons walk on two legs and raise their arms to keep their balance. This young gibbon is using his arms for balance as he walks.

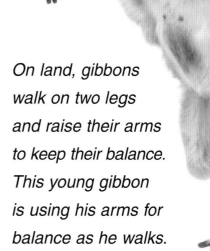

17

Lemurs and others

Lemurs belong to a group of primates called prosimians. There are many kinds of lemurs. All lemurs live on the island of Madagascar. The island is part of the **continent** of Africa. A continent is one of seven huge areas of land on Earth.

Africa

Madagascar

Ruffed lemurs live in trees and eat fruit. They have two to three babies at a time. These babies are hanging on to their mother's body.

Ring-tailed lemurs are the best-known lemurs. They have long, bushy, striped tails. These lemurs live on the ground.

Other prosimians

Lorises, bush babies, and tarsiers are other kinds of prosimians. They do not live on the island of Madagascar. Bushbabies live in other parts of Africa, and lorises and tarsiers live in Southeast Asia.

Bush babies have large eyes and ears that help them find insects in the dark.

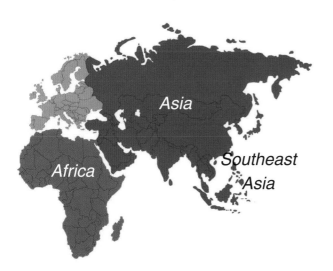

Asia

Africa

Southeast Asia

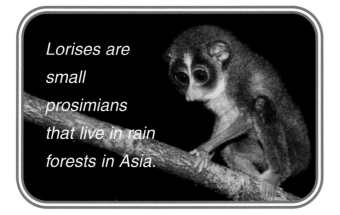

Lorises are small prosimians that live in rain forests in Asia.

Tarsiers live in Southeast Asia. They are the smallest primates. Tarsiers can turn their heads all the way around to look behind themselves. They eat insects.

19

Endangered primates

Many primates are **endangered**, or in danger of disappearing from Earth forever. Most gorillas are **critically endangered**. Critically endangered animals are at a very high risk of dying out.

Habitat loss

The biggest threat to all primates is the loss of their habitats. People are cutting down the forests where they live. Without forests, they have no shelter and no food to eat.

Threat from hunters

Baby monkeys and apes are trapped and sold as pets. Adult primates are often hunted for their meat and other body parts.

Douc langur monkeys and many other primates are endangered because they are losing their forest homes.

All gorillas are endangered, but mountain gorillas, like the mother and her baby on the right, are among the most endangered animals in the world. They are losing their habitat, and many are trapped and killed by people.

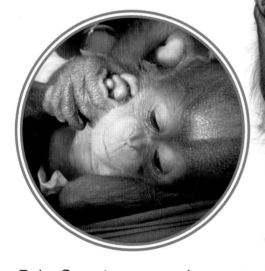

Baby Sumatran orangutans are critically endangered because of habitat loss and because they are so cute. People trap them as pets, but the babies cannot live without their mothers. They become very sad and sick.

baby Sumatran orangutan

Black-and-white ruffed lemurs are critically endangered because their habitats are almost gone. Without the fruits that grow in these habitats, baby lemurs like these may starve to death.

Match them up

Test yourself to see how much you remember about the primates in this book. Match the pictures of these baby primates to the clues below.

A. bonobo

1. Which primate is a New World monkey?
2. Name five primates that live mainly on the ground.
3. Which primate has a padded bottom?
4. Which primate is also known as a pygmy chimpanzee?
5. Which is the smartest primate of all?
6. Which two primates are critically endangered?

B. mountain gorilla

C. golden lion tamarin

D. human

E. ring-tailed lemur

F. Sumatran orangutan

G. baboon

H. chimpanzee

23

Words to know and Index

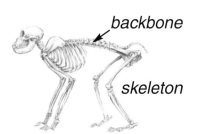

backbone

skeleton

gibbons
pages
7, 16,
17

apes
pages 7, 11,
16–17, 20

bodies
pages 4, 5,
8–9, 15, 18

chimpanzees
pages 7, 8,
16, 17, 22, 23

gorillas
pages
7, 11,
16, 20,
21, 22

habitats
pages
10–11,
20, 21

humans
pages 4, 7,
11, 21, 23

Other index words

endangered primates
    pages 20–21, 22

lemurs
pages
5, 7, 18,
21, 23

lungs
page 9

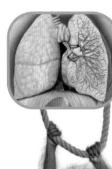

food pages 4, 5, 16, 20

mammals pages 4–5, 8

mothers pages 4, 5, 10,
    14, 16, 17, 18, 21

Old World monkeys
    pages 6, 12–13, 14

New World monkeys
    pages 6, 14–15, 22

nursing page 5

prosimians pages 7, 18–19

warm-blooded page 9

monkeys
pages 6, 8, 10,
12–15, 16,
17, 20, 22

orangutans
pages 4,
7, 11, 16,
21, 23